Lee Canter's

What To Do
When Your
Child Needs To

STUDY

Helping Your Child Master
Test-Taking and Study Skills

Lee Canter's Effective Parenting Books

Written by Patricia Sarka
Designed by Bob Winberry
Illustrations by Patty Briles

Editorial Staff
Marlene Canter
Jacqui Hook
Barbara Schadlow
Kathy Winberry

Printed in the United States of America
First printing March 1994

98 97 96 95 94   10 9 8 7 6 5 4 3 2 1

ISBN #0-939007-83-5

Sound familiar?

Do you remember when you first taught your child how to tie her shoes, ride a bike or write his name? With much love and patience, you practiced these techniques with your child over and over again until the skill was mastered.

We are continually teaching our children how to do this or how to do that, yet we often don't teach them some of the basic study skills that can mean the difference between success and failure in school. These skills don't come naturally. They must be taught and practiced. This book will help you teach these study skills to your child.

SUPER STUDY SKILLS

HELP KIDS LEARN

What are study skills anyway?

According to the *American Heritage Children's Dictionary*, "Studying is the act or process of learning something." When your child is given an assignment to study spelling words, study for a math test, or study a chapter in the history book, does he know how to best go about learning the material? Many children don't have the faintest idea of how to tackle an assignment or prepare for a test. And without these skills, they probably won't be as successful as they could on their nightly assignments and tests.

Your child needs a comprehensive study plan and that's what this book is all about.

This book is divided into five sections, each one focusing on simple techniques to help your child **learn how to study**. From early elementary through senior high school, children are expected to study and master many skills: math facts and computation skills; spelling, grammar and punctuation; geography, history, science and health. In junior and senior high school, students study a variety of subjects, learning from classroom lectures and textbooks. When your child is equipped with the right study tools, the road to mastery will be a smoother ride.

When your child studies for a test, he must pull together information from many sources: class lectures, textbook assignments, homework, resource books and past quizzes. What an organizational nightmare! This book will help you work with your child to organize materials and master the study techniques that will ultimately make test-study less stressful and help your child do his very best on tests.

Here's what you'll find in this book:

Section 1
How to Take
Terrific Notes in Class

Your child's teacher gives lots of information in class lectures, but how much of this information is remembered a week or so later when test time comes, or when your child needs the information for writing a paper? This section teaches your child how to listen and take notes during class. Included in this section are speed-writing techniques to "speed up" the note-taking process, and memory triggers that will help your child retrieve learned information during tests.

Section 2
How to Study
from a Textbook

Textbook study is a fact of life for students, yet most children waste a lot of time reading and rereading a chapter and retaining very little. In this section your child will learn an easy-to-follow method for effectively studying any textbook chapter.

Section 3
How to Prepare
for Test Study

The tips and practice activities in this section will teach your child how to organize materials and time for test study.

Section 4
How to Study
for a Test

The guidelines included in this section will help your child learn how to review class notes and textbook notes for tests in specific subject areas such as science, history and literature. Also included are tips and ideas for studying vocabulary, spelling words and math facts.

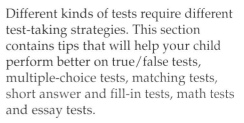

Section 5
How to Successfully
Take Tests

Different kinds of tests require different test-taking strategies. This section contains tips that will help your child perform better on true/false tests, multiple-choice tests, matching tests, short answer and fill-in tests, math tests and essay tests.

Parents Want to Know

Questions & Answers

Are you concerned that your child doesn't have the skills necessary to do his or her best on tests? Is studying done in a haphazard manner? Many parents want to help, but they don't know how. Here are some common concerns of parents just like you:

Q My son does all his homework (daily work, reports, studying for tests) while sitting on the floor in front of the TV. His grades are average, but I can't help thinking that this isn't the best place for him to work. Since he's doing OK, maybe I shouldn't rock the boat. What do you think?

ANSWER: Have you ever tried to balance your checkbook or work on your taxes in a noisy room without adequate space to work or the necessary materials you need close at hand? It makes the job tougher, doesn't it? It's just as hard for your son to do his best job studying when he's working in a noisy, distracting environment.

In order to study successfully, your child needs a quiet environment that's adequately equipped and well lit. The television should be turned off; the radio, if on at all, must be very low; and brothers and sisters should not be allowed to interrupt study time. A table (or desk) and chair are study area basics. Studying for tests requires good note-taking skills and these cannot be completed easily with your son lying on the floor. If he doesn't have a desk, suggest the kitchen table or set up a card table in his bedroom or any quiet corner of the house. Once your son gets into the habit of studying in a proper environment, his average grades will undoubtedly show marked improvement.

Q Question: Our 11-year-old daughter wastes a lot of study time searching for the materials she needs to study with. Is there an easy way to get her organized and help her get the most out of her study sessions?

ANSWER: Study-session scavenger hunts will no longer rob your child of precious study time once you put together a Study Buddy Survival Kit for her. This kit is a collection of all the materials needed to study at home: pencils, erasers, index cards, lined paper, ruler, markers, highlighter, Post It™ notes, paper clips, dictionary, etc. Place these study materials in a shoe box (plastic container, desk drawer) and put it in her study area. When she needs to make flash cards, the necessary materials (index cards, markers) will be right at her fingertips. Remind your daughter to let you know when supplies need to be refilled. And remember to refrain from using these supplies for other family needs.

Q Since our sons entered middle school they are required to take more tests than ever before. How can we fit test-study time into their hectic daily schedules—soccer practice, orthodontic visits, chores and homework?

ANSWER: A busy schedule requires planning and communication. Sit down with your sons at the beginning of the week and jot down a list of scheduled activities and responsibilities for the upcoming week. Write these activities and their times on a weekly calendar. Next, discuss any upcoming tests and then set aside adequate time each night for your children to study for these tests (making notes, reviewing notes, working with flash cards, being quizzed by parent). Your child will learn more by reviewing 15 or 20 minutes every night rather than cramming test-study time into several hours the night before a test.

Hints: A test-study planning sheet will help your sons organize the materials they need to study. (See page 33 for specific details.) Also consider purchasing an inexpensive wipe-off wall calendar. It's the perfect way to schedule study time for those big tests and midterms that require many weeks of preparation and review.

Q I'm tired of nagging my daughter to study for her weekly spelling tests. What's the best way to motivate a child who hates to study?

ANSWER: It could be that your daughter procrastinates because she simply doesn't know how to study. Create a study plan that she can follow to master her spelling words.

For example, on Monday night give her a test to determine which words she already knows. Then make flash cards for the words she has difficulty with. Have her say and spell the words aloud, trace them with her finger, and then write them on a chalkboard. On Tuesday, play a spelling game with letter tiles. Practice with the flash cards. On Wednesday, give her an oral test and then have her write all misspelled words five times each. On Thursday evening, play Beat the Clock. See how quickly she can write all her spelling words. Write the time on her paper. Then do it again to see if she can beat the time.

Your positive attitude, praise and continued support for her daily study efforts will also motivate her to study. Your job is to make her feel good about studying. You need to praise her efforts and occasionally offer her special incentives for studying on a regular basis.

Before You Begin
Some Study Basics

Throughout this book you will learn techniques that will help your child study more effectively. To make the most of these skills, here are a few study basics to keep in mind:

Your child needs a proper **study area** in which to work.

Your child can't be expected to study in the midst of family conversations, arguments over TV, or ongoing brother-and-sister debates about anything and everything. In order to study successfully your child needs a quiet space in which to work. It doesn't really matter where a child studies as long as the location is quiet and well lit. The kitchen table, a bedroom, or a corner of the living room can be great places to study as long as the study area is free from distractions that can interrupt your child's concentration. Keep noise levels down by asking all family members to "turn down the volume" during study time.

Your child needs an **assignment book**.

One of the keys to completing homework and studying for tests is to write down all assignments as they are given. A weekly assignment book is the perfect way for your child to keep track of these assignments. This is also a great way for you to keep informed of daily assignments and upcoming tests.

Your child needs to **schedule study time**.

Unless study time is scheduled, it often places last on your child's "to do" list. Encourage your child to set aside time each day just to study. During this time all other activities should stop: no TV, no phone, no visits from friends. Scheduling study time is easy. First, purchase or create a weekly schedule. Then have your child write down all after-school activities for the week (sports practice, music lessons, household jobs, etc.). From the time available, have your child choose a block of free time each day and designate it for studying.

Your child needs appropriate **study supplies** close at hand.

Once your child settles down to work you don't want her interrupted by having to search for a pencil, index cards, or any other necessary study supplies. Make sure all homework and study supplies are close at hand by obtaining all the materials needed to study and then putting them in a special place (shoe box, plastic container, desk drawer). A complete study kit includes: 3-ring binder, 3-hole lined paper, pencils, erasers, ruler, index cards, assignment book, highlighter, paper clips, and dictionary.

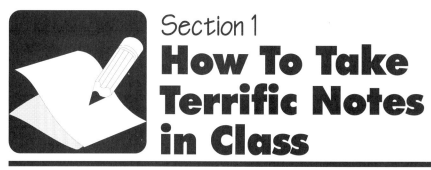

Section 1
How To Take Terrific Notes in Class

Note taking is one of the most useful study skills your child will ever learn. Too often, however, students take notes haphazardly. They either write down too much, not enough or become hopelessly lost and give up altogether. Help your child master the art of good note taking by teaching the following 3-step skill:

STEP 1

Taking Notes in Class

Pages 12 - 18

STEP 2

The 3Rs of Reviewing Class Notes

Pages 19 - 20

STEP 3

The 4th R: Remembering Class Notes with Memory Triggers

Pages 21 - 26

Taking Notes in Class

Note taking isn't just a skill for junior and senior high school students. As early as third and fourth grade, students are expected to listen to lectures in class. They'll learn more (and do better on tests and written reports) if they learn to become good note takers. Here's how:

Prepare Your Notebook

In order to take good notes, your child will need the following materials:

- A loose-leaf binder with 8.5"x 11" sheets of lined paper
- Several pencils with erasers
- A ruler

Notes	Memory Triggers
The moon–2160 mi. dia. is 1 of lrgst. in slr systm.	
Closest mn. cms to erth is 252,463 mi.	
1st man/mn–Neal Armstrong 7-20-69	

Sample Note-Taking Page

Show your child how to create a note-taking page.

1) Use a ruler to draw a vertical line about 2 inches from the right margin of the lined paper as shown.

2) The space to the left of the line is for taking notes.

3) The space to the right of line is called the **Memory Trigger margin**. (You will be given ideas for the margin later on.)

Now have your child make some note-taking pages. Place completed sheets in your child's notebook or binder.

8 Terrific Tips for Taking Notes in Class!

These tips will help your child take great notes. Go over each one with your child.

TIP #1:   Listen carefully to the teacher and concentrate on what is being said.

TIP #2:   When you hear important facts or ideas, write them down in the Notes area of your paper.

TIP #3:   Write the information in simple sentences or paragraphs.

TIP #4:   Write down details and examples, too. This kind of information is often asked on quizzes and tests.

TIP #5:   Write as quickly and as neatly as you can.

TIP #6:   Use abbreviations and symbols when possible. (See pages 14 and 15.)

TIP #7:   Use a speed-writing system to increase your note-taking speed. (See pages 14-18.)

TIP #8:   Ask questions when you need more explanation.

Use *Speed-Writing* Shortcuts

The more quickly your child can take notes in class, the more information she will have to study later. The most successful note takers record more information with less writing by using speed-writing techniques.

Speed-Writing Shortcut #1
Using Symbols

A symbol is a mark or sign that represents something. Lots of time can be saved by using symbols instead of words when taking notes.

Here are some examples of common symbols:

$	dollars
¢	cents
&	and
#	pound
%	percent
+	plus
−	minus
=	is equal to
<	is less than
>	is greater than
x	multiply
*	important

Speed-Writing Shortcut #2
Using Beginning Letters

This is another shortcut that's easy to use because your child decides where to abbreviate and end the word. This is a good method to use for words that are written over and over again. For example, if your child knows that Pres. means President, she doesn't need to spend time writing the whole word.

Here are some examples of shortened words:

ans. _____	answer
bio. _____	biography
com. ____	complete
def. ____	definition
dir. _____	directions
expl. ___	explain
imp. ____	important
inf. _____	information
para. ___	paragraph
prob. ___	problem
proj. ____	project
ques. ___	question(s)
sent. ___	sentence
sub. _____	subtract

Speed-Writing Shortcut #3 **Using Abbreviations**

An **abbreviation** is a short way of writing a word or a group of words. By using abbreviations for states, countries, directions, days of the week, months of the year and so on, your child will be able to take notes faster and easier. Here are some examples of common abbreviations.

COMMON ABBREVIATIONS

Days of the Week

M.	Monday
T.	Tuesday
W.	Wednesday
Th.	Thursday
F.	Friday
S.	Saturday
Sun.	Sunday

Months of the Year

Jan.	January
Feb.	February
Mar.	March
Apr.	April
Aug.	August
Sep.	September
Oct.	October
Nov.	November
Dec.	December

States

AL	Alabama
AK	Alaska
AZ	Arizona
CA	California
CO	Colorado
CT	Connecticut
DE	Delaware

DC	District of Columbia
FL	Florida
GA	Georgia
GU	Guam
HI	Hawaii
ID	Idaho
IL	Illinois
IN	Indiana
IA	Iowa
KS	Kansas
KY	Kentucky
LA	Louisiana
ME	Maine
MD	Maryland
MA	Massachusetts
MI	Michigan
MN	Minnesota
MS	Mississippi
MO	Missouri
MT	Montana
NE	Nebraska
NV	Nevada
NH	New Hampshire
NJ	New Jersey
NM	New Mexico
NY	New York
NC	North Carolina
ND	North Dakota
OH	Ohio

OK	Oklahoma
OR	Oregon
PA	Pennsylvania
PR	Puerto Rico
RI	Rhode Island
SC	South Carolina
SD	South Dakota
TN	Tennessee
TX	Texas
UT	Utah
VT	Vermont
VA	Virginia
VI	Virgin Islands
WA	Washington
WV	West Virginia
WI	Wisconsin
WY	Wyoming

Weights and Measures

in	inch
ft	foot
yd	yard
mi	mile
mm	millimeter
cm	centimeter
dm	decimeter
m	meter
km	kilometer

Speed-Writing Shortcut #4

Deleting Vowels and Silent Letters

Your child will love this speed-writing technique because it's so easy to use. The only thing your child has to remember is to leave out the vowels and silent letters when writing words. This technique becomes even easier the more it is practiced.

Here are some examples:

book .... becomes: **bk**

write .... becomes: **rt**

read .... becomes: **rd**

paper .... becomes: **ppr**

notebook ... becomes: **ntbk**

health .... becomes: **hlth**

folder .... becomes: **fldr**

tomorrow .. becomes: **tmrow**

homework .. becomes: **hmwrk**

project .... becomes: **prjkt**

report .... becomes: **rprt**

label .... becomes: **lbl**

theme .... becomes: **thm**

compare .... becomes: **cmpr**

prefix .... becomes: **prfx**

perimeter ... becomes: **prmtr**

Keep in mind that if a word contains an important sounded vowel (especially when it's the first letter of the word), you may choose to leave it in. The letters "bk" could stand for book, bike, buck, bake or back. If the word seems confusing without the vowel, write it in.

Adlt bks ft fr fmls.

This sentence is easier to decode if written:

Adlt buks fit fr femls.

Here are more examples:

astronaut ...... becomes: **astrnt**

volcano .... becomes: **vlcno**

interview ...... becomes: **ntrvu**

rainbow .... becomes: **ranbo**

⭐ These speed-writing techniques can also be helpful when taking notes from textbooks.

Parent-Child Activity

Practice Speed-Writing Session

Give your child some practice with this speed-writing technique. First, have your child decode these words.

pn & pncl _____

orgniz _____

ppr clp _____

clr dy _____

rd & rit _____

Now have your child decode these sentences.

I nd a rlr & a cmps fr my hmwrk tdy.

_____

_____

_____

Actns spk ldr thn wrds.

_____

_____

_____

_____

Practice Session Using
All Speed-Writing Shortcuts

Read aloud a paragraph from one of your child's textbooks. In the
space below, have your child take notes on the paragraph using the
speed-writing techniques discussed in this section. When completed,
have your child read the notes to you.

STEP 2 The 3Rs of Reviewing Class Notes

For the past month at school your child has been learning about the early explorers. Each day he has taken notes in class. Now the teacher announces an upcoming test.

What's the best course of action?

Get out the notes!

Your child's class notes can be a great study guide for the upcoming test as long as the 3Rs of reviewing class notes are followed:

1. Reread.
2. Rewrite.
3. Reinforce.

Study Buddies

It will be helpful for your child to have a **study buddy** to help review class notes. Your child's partner should be someone who is interested in the subject and cares about being an equal study partner.

Classmates make great study buddies. Encourage your child to invite his study buddy home for afternoon or early-evening study sessions. If home study isn't possible, allow your child to study by phone with his study buddy.

If your child doesn't have a classmate to study with, *you* (or a brother or sister) can become your child's study partner. Even younger siblings can help—especially with flash-card study.

Reread

The first step is to reread the notes aloud. If your child is working with a study buddy, they should read the same section of notes aloud to each other. Repeating the information aloud will help commit it to memory.

Rewrite

Sometimes notes written quickly in class can be difficult to read and understand later. While the information is still fresh in your child's mind have him rewrite notes that are scribbled or unclear. Working with a study buddy is a great idea at this time. If one forgets an important point, the other may be able to fill in the information.

Reinforce

To reinforce means to strengthen by adding something. Your child can strengthen his class notes by adding important, relevant information from his textbook. (See pages 27-31 for more information.) Once new information is added, have your child use a high-lighter pen to spotlight important facts and information. Here are some ideas:

- Underline main ideas.
- Place an asterisk (*) by important names.
- Circle important dates or facts.

This is a sample of speed-writing notes taken during a science class.

| Jimmy | Science Notes | Oct. 15 |

Vertebrates
* mamls, fsh, brds, repls, amfbns
—Ver. hav bran encl n branpn & seg spnl clm (bkbn)
—Bkbn—thk crd of nrv tsu of centrl nrvs sys
Bones cald vertebrae.
Humn vert. names (tp-btm)—7 cervical, 12 thoracic, 5 lumbar, 5 sacral (fused) 4 coccygeal (fused)

This is a sample of notes that has been rewritten, using reinforcers to emphasize important information.

| Jimmy | Science Notes | Oct. 15 |

Notes on <u>Vertebrates</u>
These animals are (all vertebrates:)
* mammals
* fish
* birds
* reptiles
* amphibians
Vertebrates have:
* a <u>brain</u> enclosed <u>in a brainpan</u>
* a <u>segmented spinal column</u> or (backbone)

The (spinal column) is a <u>thick cord of nerve tissue</u> of the <u>central nervous system</u>.

These are bones that make up the (spinal column) (from top to bottom):
* 7 <u>cervical</u> vertebrae
* 12 <u>thoracic</u>
* 5 <u>lumbar</u>
* 5 <u>sacral</u> (these bones are fused)
* 4 <u>coccygeal</u> (also fused)

STEP 3
The 4th R:
Remembering Class Notes with
Memory Triggers

The brain stores many memories. Some of these memories may seem forgotten until something or someone triggers the memory to come alive again. Your child can create her own memory triggers to help remember ideas, facts, names, dates and other information from her notes. These memory devices should be written in the right-hand margin of your child's note-taking page.

Notes	Memory Triggers
The moon-2160 mi. dia. is 1 of lrgst. in slr systm.	2160
Closest mn. cms to erth is 252,463 mi.	252,436
1 st man/mn-Neal Armstrong 7-20-69	7-20-69

A **memory trigger** can be a word, phrase or picture. The key is to find the memory tricks that work best. We have included a few ideas to help your child get started. (See pages 22 - 26.)

Memory Trigger #1
Dates and Rhymes

Dates and facts can be memorized in no time when they are paired with rhymes.

In 1492,
Columbus sailed the ocean blue.

1775 was the year
Of that famous ride of Paul Revere.

On July 20th of 1969
Neil Armstrong took a
giant leap for mankind.

Have your child make up memory trigger rhymes for these important dates in U.S. History:

Boston Tea Party in 1773

_____

_____

California Gold Rush begins in 1849

_____

_____

_____

Memory Trigger #2
Picture This!

They say that a picture is worth a thousand words. Sometimes drawing a simple picture can help trigger information later when it's needed at test time!

Example: If you need to remember that Neal Armstrong was the first person to step on the moon on July 20, 1969, just draw a picture. You might draw a kneeling (for Neal) astronaut, his arm muscle flexing (for Armstrong), on the moon, holding an American flag. The date can be written on the drawing.

Neal Armstrong 7-20-69

Once the memory trigger is finished, study the picture carefully, closing your eyes and visualizing the picture and memorizing the details.

Have your child sketch a memory trigger picture for each of the following:

Giant sequoia trees have lived for as long as 4,000 years.

The Pilgrims arrived in America aboard the Mayflower in 1620.

Secret Sentence Codes!

At some time during your child's school years, she will surely be asked to memorize a list of names or words: the continents, the planets, presidents. By creating a sentence code, your child will be able to remember the information in correct order. Here's how it works:

1. List the words you want to remember in the order that you want to remember them.

   Example: You need to memorize the five largest oceans of the world. They are (in order of size) the Pacific, Atlantic, Indian, Arctic and Mediterranean Sea.

2. Underline the first letter of each word.

   <u>P</u>acific, <u>A</u>tlantic, <u>I</u>ndian, <u>A</u>rctic and <u>M</u>editerranean Sea.

   (P, A, I, A, M)

3. Now make up a sentence using the words that begin with the same letter on your list.

   Penguins **A**dore **I**cebergs **A**nd **M**ollusks.

Memory trigger sentences are most effective when the secret code creates a mental picture of your subject. Penguins, icebergs, and mollusks can all be found in the ocean.)

You probably remember some memory triggers that have helped you—even through your adult life. Here are some common memory triggers that your child may find helpful:

Colors of the rainbow (in order)
Memory Trigger — ROY G. BIV
Red, Orange, Yellow, Green, Blue, Indigo, Violet

Names of the Great Lakes
Memory Trigger — HOMES
Huron, Ontario, Michigan, Erie, Superior

How to spell "arithmetic"
Memory Trigger —Remember this sentence
A Rat In The House Might Eat The Ice Cream

Confusing spellings — "desert" "dessert"
Memory Trigger—Remember that the 2 "s's" in de<u>ss</u>ert mean "something sweet" and the one "s" in de<u>s</u>ert is "sand."

Confusing spellings — "principal" "principle"
Memory Trigger—Remember that the princi<u>pal</u> is your <u>pal</u>.

Have your child create secret sentence codes for these facts:

The first five presidents of the U.S.: Washington, Adams, Jefferson, Madison, Monroe

_____

_____

_____

_____

_____

_____

_____

Planets (in order from the sun): Mercury, Venus, Earth, Mars, Jupiter, Saturn, Uranus, Neptune, Pluto

_____

_____

_____

_____

_____

_____

_____

_____

How to Use Memory Triggers

Look at the notebook paper your child prepared with the Memory Trigger column. Explain to your child that she should use this column to write memory trigger rhymes or sentences or to sketch memory trigger pictures that will help touch off reminders about the information in her notes. When studying her notes, your child should use the memory trigger to help her recite the information in the Notes area.

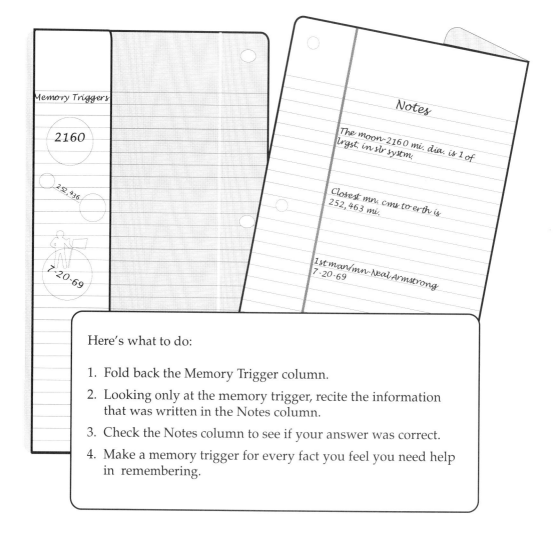

Here's what to do:

1. Fold back the Memory Trigger column.

2. Looking only at the memory trigger, recite the information that was written in the Notes column.

3. Check the Notes column to see if your answer was correct.

4. Make a memory trigger for every fact you feel you need help in remembering.

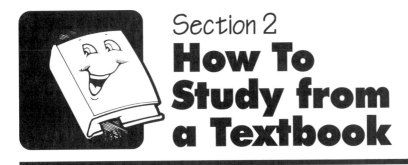

Section 2
How To Study from a Textbook

Children often spend many unproductive hours trying to study their textbooks. They read and reread but then don't remember a thing. This doesn't have to be the case.

First, help your child get acquainted with his textbook.

Textbooks can be very intimidating to children. Help your child overcome his textbook phobias by introducing him to the various and extremely helpful parts of each book (see page 28). Most texts are actually designed to help the reader study, so by familiarizing himself with these parts, your child will understand the material better and thus be a more successful student.

Then, adopt a textbook study system.

Your child will get more out of his nightly textbook study sessions if he follows the simple 4-step plan outlined in this section. This system will help your child remember more of what he reads and that will be a great advantage at test-taking time.

Getting Acquainted with the Textbook

The purpose of a textbook is to instruct the reader in a particular subject: history, language, math, science, etc. From beginning to end, it is jam-packed with important information—names, dates, places, facts, ideas, theories and formulas. Reading a textbook doesn't have to be difficult, as long as the reader understands that reading a textbook is different from reading a book for pleasure.

Let's first look at how a textbook is organized.

Unlike most other books, a textbook is divided into sections and chapters, with headings and subheadings. Textbooks might also contain pictures and maps, charts and graphs, summaries and questions, special word lists, a glossary and an index.

As you read the list on the next page, notice how all the parts of the textbook can be used to study more effectively. This is the point you want your child to understand: A textbook is designed to do more than contain lots of information. It is specifically designed to help your child study and learn that information.

Valuable Parts
of a Textbook

Table of Contents

This quick reference is found in the front of a textbook. It provides a simple outline of what is included in the book.

By reading the Table of Contents your child will know what the book covers.

Chapter Headings & Subheadings

These titles provide an overview of the information to be covered in each chapter.

Chapter Summaries

These short reviews are found at the end of each chapter. A helpful technique is to read each chapter summary *before* studying the chapter. This preview explains what the author thinks are the most important ideas presented in the chapter.

Chapter Questions

The quickest way to find out what specific information the author wants you to remember from the chapter is to read these questions first. Pay particular attention to names, dates, and specific details.

Word Lists

These lists of special terms need special attention. Your child should be aware of these words when reading the chapter. If the author feels they are important enough to be singled out, then so should the reader.

Glossary

This textbook dictionary lists many words and names mentioned throughout the book.

Index

When you need to locate specific information fast, use the index in the back of the book. This alphabetized list of terms, names and events will help the reader locate the page on which the information can be found.

Teach Your Child
the 4-Step Textbook Study Method

The child who masters this study technique early in her school years will have a much easier time when she reaches junior and senior high school. All she needs are her textbook, paper and pencil and these four steps.

Scan

Give the chapter a quick lookover by spot reading certain parts of the chapter. Depending on the length of the chapter, this step should take from 5 to 15 minutes.

Scanning will give your child a quick but in-depth overview of everything that's contained in the textbook chapter.

Here's how to scan:

- Read the **title of the chapter** and each **heading** and **subheading**.
- Read the **opening paragraph** of the chapter.
- Read the **first paragraph** of each new heading.
- Read the **first sentence** of all other paragraphs.
- Read the **chapter summary**.
- Read the **chapter questions**.
- Scan all **pictures**, **maps**, **charts** and other **visual aids**. Read any **captions**.

Chunk and Read

Does your child ever feel overwhelmed by a textbook reading assignment? If the task seems too big, some children give up before they begin. The answer to this problem is **chunking**.

Chunking means dividing a chapter into smaller, more manageable, bite-size pieces or paragraphs. Each paragraph in a chapter contains important information the author wants the reader to learn. In order to get the most out of this interesting feast, your child needs to consume each paragraph slowly, chewing on the words, getting a taste of what the author is saying, savoring the important facts and information and then digesting it.

Heres how to "chunk and read":

- Instead of reading page after page without stopping, your child should **read one paragraph at a time**.
- After reading each paragraph, your child should pause and ask herself this question:

What idea or information was the author trying to get across to me in this paragraph?

- When she can complete this statement,

"The author is saying _____

_____

in this paragraph," then she is ready to go on to the next paragraph.

STEP 3 Recall and Record

Once your child has completed chunking and reading a page, it's time for her to **recall** what was said in each paragraph and **record** this information on paper. Like class notes, textbook notes should be written on lined paper that has been prepared with a vertical line 2 inches from the right margin. (See sample.)

Write questions about important dates, places, or events. After completing the questions and answers for the first paragraph, your child should skip a line and follow the same steps for the rest of the paragraphs on the page.

Your child should follow these steps when recalling and recording information from *each page* of the textbook.

- **Reread** the first paragraph on the page.
- Write the **page number and paragraph numbers** in the *left* margin.
- Compose **questions** from the information presented in the paragraph and write them in the *middle* column. (No true/false or multiple-choice questions.)
- Write the **answers** to the questions in the *right-hand* column.

If new terms or vocabulary words are introduced in the paragraph, write a definition question. (For example: What is a mammal?)

Pg. Ref	Question about information	Answer
p24 ¶3	What is a hurricane?	tropical cyclone
p23 ¶4	How great an area does a hurricane cover?	200 - 400 miles diameter
p23 ¶4	What is the wind velocity of a hurricane?	over 74 m.p.h
	What was the wind velocity of hurricane Camille in 1969?	over 172 m.p.h
p24 ¶3	What are hurricanes in the western Pacific called?	typhoons

STEP 4 Recite

After scanning, chunking, recalling and recording the entire chapter, it's time to recite from memory the information learned in the chapter.

Here's what your child needs to do:

1. Close the textbook.

2. Take out the **notebook** pages of questions and answers from the assigned chapter reading. Fold back the right-hand margin so the answers can't be seen.

3. Read each **question** and then say the answer out loud. (Parent can read questions and check answers.)

4. If your child is unable to answer the question, she should open the textbook to the page and paragraph referenced by the question. Then she should **reread** the paragraph and **find the answer**. Have her read the information aloud.

5. As each question is answered correctly, have your child **make a check mark** next to the answer.

6. Your child should **answer** each question on the note pages.

7. Before a test, these questions and answers should be **reviewed** several times.

If your child follows these steps when a chapter is first assigned for reading, test study will not be an overwhelming task.

"I can't study tonight because I left my textbook in my locker."

Your child may occasionally leave a textbook at school. Everybody makes mistakes once in a while. But if your child is a chronic "forgetter", you need to step in and take action.

1. Make sure your child has a backpack or book bag in which to bring books back and forth from school.

2. Give your child a homework assignment book in which to jot down all assignments. Have him put check marks by all assignments that will require a textbook. Before leaving school at the end of the day, he should review assignments and place all necessary books in his backpack.

3. Talk to your child about the problem. Give him a choice of bringing home the necessary textbooks or losing privileges (such as phone or television privileges).

"Because you have homework in math every night, you must remember to bring your book home. The next time you forget your textbook, you'll lose your phone and television privileges for the night."

* This is especially useful for the chronic textbook forgetter.

Section 3
How To Prepare for Test Study

Test!

This word can spell panic for young and old alike. Spelling test, multiplication facts quiz, history final, driver's test, placement exam. Just the thought of a test makes many of us anxious and upset. But it doesn't have to be that way. Most test terrors and quiz crazies can be eliminated with proper test preparation. The following guidelines will help your child prepare for tests and eliminate those pre-test panic attacks.

Test-Study Preparation Tip #1
Schedule study and review sessions on a regular basis.

To be prepared on test day, your child should set aside some time each week to review class and textbook notes. Younger children who need drilling on spelling words or math facts should also set aside 10 to 15 minutes each day to practice. Reviewing and practicing on a regular basis is a must. If your child complains about these regular practice sessions, explain that good habits bring good results. You might say:

"Brushing and flossing your teeth every day will pay off when you get a clean bill of health from the dentist. But no matter how much you brush and floss the night before your dental appointment, you can never make up for the time you neglected your teeth. You need to keep brushing up on your skills on a regular basis."

At the beginning of the week (Monday night) talk to your child about upcoming assignments. Are any tests scheduled? If so, your child should plan some study and review sessions. If a test is announced during the week, make sure your child records it in his assignment book and schedules adequate study sessions.

Test-Study Preparation Tip #2
Find out what the test will cover.

Before your child can study for a test, he needs to know what material the test will cover. If the teacher does not explain exactly what will be covered on the test, encourage your child to ask. Will the test cover:

- Spelling words only or dictation sentences?

- Subtraction facts only or computation problems?

- Science formulas or vocabulary words?

- Textbook material and/or lecture material?

- Any past quizzes or tests?

- Homework assignments?

All information about the upcoming test should be recorded on the Test-Study Planner (see page 45). This sheet will guide your child through his test-study sessions. Your child should also list any specific material or information he may need to know—formulas, states and capitals, grammar rules, etc.

TEST-STUDY PLANNER

Subject to be tested __Science__ Test date __3/02__

TYPE OF TEST
- ☐ short answer
- ☑ fill-in
- ☐ true/false
- ☐ multiple-choice
- ☐ matching
- ☐ essay
- ☐ reading comprehension
- ☐ math computation
- ☐ other ____

WHAT THE TEST WILL COVER
The ideas, facts, information and other material I need to know for this test include:

Notes on field trip to shore.

Names and types of seashells,

Shore birds, spawning, fish eggs.

THE MATERIAL I NEED TO STUDY
In the spaces below, I have listed all the specific material I need to study for this test. When the specific material has been studied and learned, I will check it off.

Textbook Chapter # or Title	Page(s)	Completed
10, Life at the Seashore	10-19	

Class Notes from (date) __2/10__ to (date) __2/21__

Homework Assignments __Seashell identification sheet__

Past Quizzes/Tests __None__

Other Materials __Seashell book__

STUDY SCHEDULE

Date/Time	Date/Time	Date/Time
2/27 8pm	2/28 7pm	3/01 7pm

Test-Study
Preparation Tip #3

Organize test-study materials.

Has anyone seen the binder with my history notes?

Mom, where are my subtraction flash cards?

Your child's study time will be more effective if he has organized all the material that will be covered on the upcoming test. For younger children these materials may include flash cards for math facts or spelling and vocabulary words. For older children it may include class and textbook notes, previous tests and quizzes, and homework assignments.

Here is an efficient way to organize test-study materials:

- Gather everything needed to study for a specific test and place it in a file folder or large manila envelope.

- Staple or tape the Test-Study Planner (page 45) to the outside of the folder or envelope.

Test-Study
Preparation Tip #4

Set the scene for study.

Studying for a test requires concentration, organization and motivation. When it's test-study time, your child should do the following:

- Turn off the radio and TV.

- Remove himself from the rest of the family (unless a family member is helping as your child's study buddy partner).

- Unplug telephone in the study area.

- Get out test-study folder or envelope containing relevant materials.

- Set a goal to study for a specific amount of time.

- Switch on a positive attitude.

- Get ready to succeed!

Section 4
How To Study for a Test

Studying for a test should be like rehearsing for a play. An actor wouldn't wait until the night before the performance to begin learning his lines and your child shouldn't wait until the night before a test to begin studying. The more you rehearse for a performance, the more confidence you have in your success. The more you study for a test, the more confidence you have that you will be successful.

If your child has completed all homework assignments, listened in class, taken good notes, studied and taken notes from the textbook and scheduled frequent review sessions, she is ready for an official **test study session**. Depending on the type of test, your child will need these materials:

- flash cards (blank cards for notes and questions; prepared cards for math, spelling, vocabulary practice)
- class lecture notes
- textbook study notes
- past quizzes or tests
- homework assignments
- blank paper
- pencils/erasers/felt-tip markers

Some children need parent study buddies to help them through the study session by asking questions, quizzing with flash cards and participating in test-study games. Your interest and involvement can make a big difference.

Study Session Suggestion #1
Prepare flash cards to help your child study.

Your child shouldn't spend precious study time reviewing information he already knows. Flash cards are a great way for your child to study for a test. They are easily created from index cards or paper cut into smaller pieces. A question, math problem or vocabulary word can be written on one side of a card with the answer, solution or definition written on the reverse.

By quickly "flashing" through the set of cards, you can determine those facts on which your child needs to concentrate his study efforts. These cards can be pulled from the pile and worked on until they are mastered.

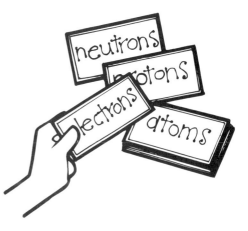

Here are some ideas for using flash cards in various subject areas:

For Math Facts, Spelling Words, Vocabulary

Give your child a quick test (using flash cards or dictating questions or problems). Set aside the flash cards (or circle any answers) to which your child gave an <u>incorrect</u> response. The remaining study time should be spent studying and mastering these facts, words or problems.

For Material Covered During Class Lectures

Have your child take out his class notes. Then have him:

1. Fold each page so that only the words, phrases and pictures in the Memory Trigger column are visible.

2. Look at each memory trigger and recite aloud what it stands for.
   - If the answer is **correct**, place a check by it.
   - If the answer is **incorrect** or your child can't remember, write the memory trigger on the front of a flash card. On the back of the flash card, write the information, fact or material that the memory trigger represents.

For Material from Textbook Study Notes

Have your child take out his textbook study notes and follow the same procedures as for class lecture notes. Your child should make flash cards for all information presented in study notes that he has not memorized.

Review homework assignments.

Flash cards should be made on any information presented in homework assignments that your child is still unsure of.

Tie up any loose ends.

If there are any special vocabulary words, technical terms or math formulas that need practice, have your child make flash cards for these too.

Now your child has a pile of flash cards that contains only the material he needs to study.

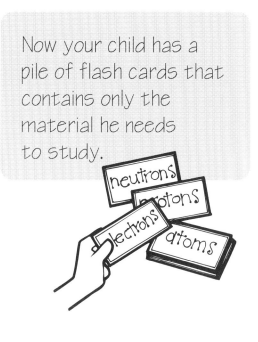

Using Flash Cards to Study

Your child has identified the material he needs to study further and has written this information on flash cards. What's next? Its time to *learn* the information, and the best way to accomplish this is the **divide and conquer** approach.

Here's how to DIVIDE AND CONQUER:

1. Divide the stack of flash cards into **four equal piles**.

2. Take the first pile and place the memory trigger/question sides face up.

3. Have your child look at the top card and study the memory trigger or read the question aloud.

4. Then your child recalls the information or gives the answer out loud.

5. The answer is checked by turning over the flash card. If the answer is correct, the flash card is placed in a discard pile. All cards placed in the discard pile contain material your child has committed to memory.

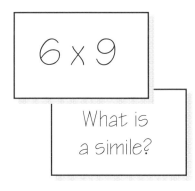

6. If your child was unable to give any answer, or if the answer was **incorrect**, reread the card again aloud. Then have your child try one or more of these ideas:

   * Create a new flash card with a better memory trigger.

   * Highlight important words.

   * Practice repeating the question and answer aloud.

   * Read the question, close your eyes, and then try to visualize the answer. Write the answer with your finger on top of your desk or table.

   This card should be placed at the bottom of the pile. You can only place a card in the discard pile when you can answer the question correctly the first time.

7. When all the cards from the first pile have been answered correctly and placed in the discard pile, praise your child for a job well done. It's time to stand up and stretch. Take a brief break, get a drink of water and then sit down.

8. Repeat the process with the second, third and fourth pile of flash cards. Don't forget to take a short break between piles. It's very important for your child to relax, stretch and clear his mind a bit.

Congratulations are in order when your child has finally mastered all four flash card piles. Hail the conquering hero with some encouraging words, a big hug and a tasty snack.

How to Help Your Child Study
Spelling Words

If your child is given a list of spelling words to learn every week, try these suggestions for making practice sessions more enjoyable and successful:

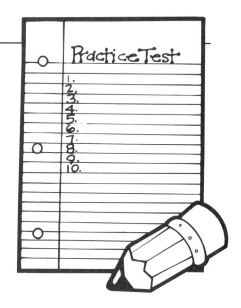

- Don't wait until the night before the test to work with your child. As with chapter tests, it's better to schedule short, nightly practices than to attempt a Thursday-night cramming session. Do a practice test of the entire list on Monday night and then work on 1/3 of the words on Tuesday, 1/3 on Wednesday and 1/3 on Thursday. A Friday morning breakfast quiz will round out the week's practice.

- Have your child write each word on a 3 x 5 flash card. Then help your child study on her own by teaching her this step-by-step system:

    1. Read the flash card word aloud and spell it.
    2. Trace the word with your finger as you spell it aloud again.

3. Use the word in a sentence.
4. Say the word and spell it aloud three times.
5. Turn over the flash card, say the word and spell it.
6. Write the word on a sheet of paper, chalkboard or wipe-off board.
7. Turn over the flash card, word side up. Check for correct spelling.
8. If correct, draw a small star on the card.
9. Repeat steps 1 to 7 if the word was spelled incorrectly.

- Flash cards, chalkboards, magnetic letters and wipe-off boards are great alternatives to paper and pencil practice.

- Encourage your child to practice words on a typewriter or computer.

Math Facts

Many a child has suffered a case of nervous stomach before and during a timed math-fact test. The quickest way to ease this anxiety is to help your child memorize these facts. Addition, subtraction, multiplication and division facts should become second nature to elementary-age students because a child who has not memorized arithmetic facts will always have a tough time in math.

> It's very important for your child to understand why 5 x 2 = 10. Use objects (coins, toothpicks, blocks) to help your child understand the arithmetic operation. For example, place 5 sets of 2 coins on the table and have your child count the total.
>
>

Here are some guidelines for teaching math facts:

⭐ Create flash cards for each set of facts (1s, 2s, 3s, 4s and so on).

⭐ Teach the lowest math facts first. (1s, 2s and so on.)

⭐ Teach those multiplication tables first that are easily counted aloud: 1s, 2s, 5s and 10s. (For example: 5, 10, 15, 20, 25, 30, 35, 40, 45)

⭐ Give your child both oral and written practice quizzes on math facts. Encourage your child to use a calculator to self-check answers on written tests.

⭐ Take baby steps when teaching math facts. Limit new facts to five a session. (1+1, 1+2, 1+3, 1+4, 1+5)

⭐ Track your child's progress on a wall chart. Reward your child for every 10 facts memorized.

⭐ Practice math facts frequently—even after your child has mastered them.

Section 5
How To Successfully Take Tests

Does your child panic at the thought of taking a test? You know she knows the material—you stayed up half the night drilling her on it. But when you ask how she did on the test, she replies, "I got so nervous that I just couldn't remember a thing."

Help your child get past her test traumas with the **7-Step Test Plan**. This general plan of attack will help your child do the best job possible on any test.

7 Steps to Success

To remember the 7 steps in the plan, have your child memorize this **memory trigger** sentence:

THE **R**ESTAURANT **S**ERVES **B**URGERS, **F**RIES, **R**ELISH, **D**ESSERT.

The first letter in each word represents one step in the plan. As soon as the test papers are handed out and the teacher says to begin, your child should follow this recipe for successful test taking.

Step 1 **T**ake 2 minutes to unload your memory bank on the back of your test papers.

For 2 minutes, and only 2 minutes, jot down all the memory triggers, names, dates, phrases, formulas and special information you can remember. When the 2 minutes are over, begin your test. When you come to a difficult question, check your "Take 2" notes. A word or picture you have scribbled on the back may trigger an answer.

Step 2 **R**ead the directions carefully.

Step 3 **S**kim the entire test quickly.

Step 4 **B**egin answering the questions.

Step 5 **F**lag any questions you cannot immediately answer and continue with the test.

Step 6 **R**eturn to the flagged questions when you have finished the last question.

- Reread the question.
- Refer to your "Take 2" notes for any pictures or words that might trigger the answer.
- If you are still stumped, try to reason out the answer.
- If all else fails, guess.

Step 7 **D**ouble-check your answers if time permits.

Tips for Successfully Taking
True/False Tests

Don't let your child fall into the trap of thinking that true/false tests are easy and don't require much study. Sure, there's a 50/50 chance of getting the answer correct just by guessing, but 50% is a failing score. By studying the right kinds of information and following these suggestions, your child should be able to perform better on this type of test.

A true/false exam tests knowledge of facts and details. The questions are usually short, but this doesn't mean that the answers are necessarily obvious.

Give your child these guidelines for taking true/false tests:

- Read the statement slowly and carefully, word by word. Remember: If any part of the statement is false, the entire statement is false. In order to be a true statement, every part must be true.

- Beware of sway words. Their very presence in a sentence can sometimes sway a statement from true to false. Some common sway words are **all, every, always, only** and **never**.

- Pay special attention to true clue words. Their presence in a sentence usually indicates that the statement is true. The most common true clue words are **usually** and **generally**.

- Stick with your first answer. Usually your first hunch is correct, so don't change an answer unless you are positive that your first choice was incorrect.

- Check your answer by rereading the statement, including your chosen answer (yes or no) as part of the statement. For example:

  True or False? Jupiter is the smallest planet in our solar system.

To check this answer you would say, **"No**, Jupiter is **not** the smallest planet in the solar system."

Tips for Successfully Taking
Multiple-Choice Tests

Multiple-choice questions are widely used in standardized tests that all children are given in school. Teachers also use this format to test information and facts. A multiple-choice question consists of two parts: a question (or an incomplete statement) followed by several possible choices. Your child's job is to choose the correct response from the choices.

Your child should follow these simple steps when taking a multiple-choice test:

1. Read the question and attempt to answer it **without** looking at the choices. If your answer is one of the choices, then you have probably chosen the correct answer.

2. Flag any question you can't answer right away and return to it after finishing the last question.

3. Read all the answer choices carefully. Often two choices will have similar answers or words.

4. Be on the lookout for **distracters**. Distracters are used to make you think a little harder. Some common distracters are words such as **everyone, all, no one, none**.

5. Eliminate choices that seem too vague or general. Correct responses are often the ones containing specific, detailed information. They may also be noticeably longer than the other choices and more carefully worded.

6. Avoid answers that seem wacky or strange. They usually are incorrect.

Multiple Choice Test

1. The Capital of California is:
   a. Los Angeles
   b. Fresno
   c. San Francisco
   d. Sacramento
   e. None of the above

Tips for Successfully Taking
Math
Tests

The following suggestions will help your child avoid some of the common pitfalls of taking math tests:

Suggestion #1

Skim the test quickly. If it requires you to use any formulas that are not given, take time to jot down those formulas on your paper.

Perimeter of a polygon $P = a + b + c$

Area of a rectangle $A = lw$

Area of a square $A = s^2$

Suggestion #2

When copying a problem onto a sheet of scratch paper, double-check the accuracy of your numbers before beginning your computation.

Suggestion #3

Draw pictures, graphs, or any visual aids that will help you visualize any problems (especially word problems) that you are having difficulty understanding.

Suggestion #4

If you are allowed to use a calculator, then use it! It will come in especially handy when you are checking your answer.

Suggestion #5

Look at the column on the right. Check each answer using the reverse method.

To check an addition problem, subtract one of the **addends** from your **sum**.

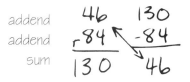

To check a subtraction problem, add your **difference** to the **minuend**. The answer should be the **subtrahend**.

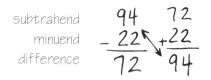

Check multiplication problems by dividing the **product** by the **quotient**.

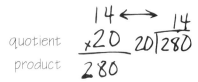

Check division problems by multiplying the **quotient** and the **divisor**.

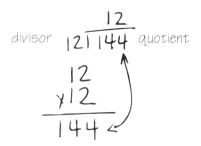

Tips for Successfully Taking
Essay Tests

An essay test is your child's chance to shine: to show what he's learned, to share his opinions; to demonstrate strong writing skills. But a good essay answer needs more than facts and ideas. The information must be well organized, thoughtfully and clearly presented in well-written sentences and paragraphs.

Here are some tips for writing a strong essay answer:

1. **Read the directions carefully.** Pay special attention to the vocabulary used in the directions.

- If a direction says **compare**, you should describe the <u>similarities</u> between two or more things, people or events.

- If a direction says **contrast**, you should describe the <u>differences</u> between two or more things, people or events.

- If a direction says **explain**, you should <u>tell about</u> or give reasons for.

- If a direction says **state**, you should briefly and concisely <u>discuss</u> a main idea or point.

- If a direction says **prove**, you should <u>give arguments</u> with facts and details <u>that support</u> a statement, point of view or theory.

- If the direction says **diagram**, you should <u>draw and label</u> a chart, graph or picture. (Your answer requires little or no written explanation.)

- If the direction says **summarize**, you should <u>sum up</u> ideas or points without getting into specific details or other unrelated information.

2. **Think before you write.** Gather your thoughts. Jot down a few notes or a quick outline. Budget your time.

3. **Begin your answer by restating the question** as a statement or by briefly answering the question.

4. **Write clear, concise sentences and use your best handwriting.**

5. **Start each paragraph with a topic sentence.** Fill your paragraphs with facts, details, opinions and other information, but don't use up the space with unnecessary information or fillers.

6. **The last paragraph should summarize the points made in the essay.**

7. **When you've finished your essay, review your work.**

TEST-STUDY PLANNER

Subject to be tested _____ Test date _____

TYPE OF TEST

☐ short answer ☐ multiple-choice ☐ reading comprehension
☐ fill-in ☐ matching ☐ math computation
☐ true/false ☐ essay ☐ other_____

WHAT THE TEST WILL COVER

The ideas, facts, information and other material I need to know for this test include:

_____

_____

_____

THE MATERIAL I NEED TO STUDY

In the spaces below, I have listed all the specific material I need to study for this test. When the specific material has been studied and learned, I will check it off.

Textbook Chapter # or Title	Page(s)	Completed

Class Notes from (date) _____ to (date) _____

Homework Assignments _____

Past Quizzes/Tests _____

Other Materials _____

STUDY SCHEDULE

Date/Time   Date/Time   Date/Time
_____   _____   _____
_____   _____   _____

TEST-STUDY PLANNER

Subject to be tested _____ Test date _____

TYPE OF TEST

☐ short answer   ☐ multiple-choice   ☐ reading comprehension
☐ fill-in   ☐ matching   ☐ math computation
☐ true/false   ☐ essay   ☐ other _____

WHAT THE TEST WILL COVER

The ideas, facts, information and other material I need to know for this test include:

_____

_____

_____

THE MATERIAL I NEED TO STUDY

In the spaces below, I have listed all the specific material I need to study for this test. When the specific material has been studied and learned, I will check it off.

Textbook Chapter # or Title   Page(s)   Completed

_____

_____

_____

Class Notes from (date) _____ to (date) _____

Homework Assignments _____

Past Quizzes/Tests _____

Other Materials _____

STUDY SCHEDULE

Date/Time   Date/Time   Date/Time

_____   _____   _____

_____   _____   _____

Lee Canter's

Top 10 Study & Test-Taking Reminders

Your program to help your child improve study and test-taking skills is underway. With your continued attention and positive motivation, your child will soon see test jitters diminishing and test scores soaring. Here are our Top Ten Study and Test-Taking Reminders to help you keep your child on track. Refer to these reminders from time to time whenever you need a quick refresher.

1. Study and test-taking skills don't come naturally to most children. These skills must be taught and practiced. If your child is not learning these skills at school, you need to teach them at home. The time you spend teaching your child study skills can make the difference between success and failure in school.

2. A proper home study environment is essential. Your child does not need a lot of space in which to study, but will do best in a quiet, well-lit location with all the necessary supplies close at hand. Ask family members to honor study time by keeping noise levels down.

3. Finding time to study doesn't have to be a problem if it's scheduled like all of the other activities in your child's life. Encourage your child to use a weekly/monthly calendar to record specific times for daily study sessions. Upcoming tests can be written on the calendar, too. By planning short, nightly study sessions rather than one intensive, night-before-the-test cramming session, your child will retain more information for the test.

4. The right study materials are essential for study success. Make sure your child has a 3-ring binder filled with lined paper, a ruler, note cards, a highlighter pen, pencils, erasers and an age-appropriate dictionary.

5. Knowing how to study a textbook chapter is essential when preparing for a test. Few children can read through a chapter once and remember all they need to know to do well on a test. Have your child scan the chapter, then chunk and read each paragraph on a page. When the page is complete, have your child recall the information from each paragraph by creating questions and answers about the material. These questions and answers serve as study sheets once the entire chapter is completed.

6. Be prepared to work hand-in-hand with your child during test-study sessions. Play simple flash card games. Ask questions. If necessary, use objects to teach (and reteach) concepts that your child may have difficulty understanding. Test anxiety will be minimized if your child has learned and practiced the material to be covered. Just remember, don't show your disappointment or become discouraged when your child has difficulty with the material. Be enthusiastic and praise your child's progress and improvement.

7. Encourage your child to use a Test-Study Planner (page 45) when preparing for upcoming tests and quizzes. Study sessions can be more productive when your child knows the type of test to be given and the material that will be covered on the test.

8. Help your child simplify the note-taking process by teaching some simple speed-writing shortcuts: using abbreviations and symbols, writing the first few letters of a word, and shortening words by deleting vowels and silent letters.

9. If your child's memory goes blank during tests, help bring those memories back to the surface with **memory triggers**. Discover the memory tricks that work best for your child. Visual learners are helped by drawing picture memory triggers. Auditory (listening) learners recall information that is set to rhymes. Memory triggers should be recorded on your child's study sheets and then practiced during study sessions.

10. Give your child a head start to test success by making sure that he or she gets adequate sleep the night before, eats a healthy meal, and has a positive, calm attitude.